stroke

poems

sidney wade

A KAREN & MICHAEL BRAZILLER BOOK
PERSEA BOOKS / NEW YORK

—for my two beautiful daughters, Amanda and Elena

Thanks to the editors of the following journals, in which these poems first appeared:

32 Poems: "In the Uncertain Light of All We've Seen"; *Autumn House Anthology of Contemporary American Poetry:* "Ants and a Little, Vicious Pig," "Insurance," "Leaving Train," "Snake"; *Bomb:* "The Body Politic," "The Visionary from Apopka"; *Cincinnati Review:* "The Weight of Light"; *Field:* "Ember," "Grand Disastery"; *Gettysburg Review:* "Deep Gossip," "No Comfort to be Had," "Sexual Blossoms and their Fierce Addictions"; *Literary Imagination:* "Poetry and Pleasure"; *New England Review:* "Insurance"; *Paris Review:* "Q.E.D.," "*Siamo a la Frutta*"; *Parthenon West Review:* "The Vulgate of Experience"; *Poets Against the War:* "Doomsday Verse"; *Southern Poetry Review:* "After the Flood, Frogs," "Pity the Poor Orange"; *Quadrant:* "Lost Words," "No Fact is a Bare Fact"; *TriQuarterly:* "A Computerized Jet Fountain in the Detroit Metro Airport," "Metaphysician in the Dark," "Metaphysician in the Light"; *Verse:* "Avant-gardening on my weeping knees," "Nothing But the Truth," "Six Significant Landscapes and Two Brief Intrigues."

Gratitude and love to Poultry Group, past, present, and extended: Lola Haskins, Brandy Kershner, Joe Haldeman, David Gehler, Jon Loomis, Geoff Brock, and Randy Mann (honorary).

Persea Books, Inc.,
853 Broadway, NYC, NY 10003

Printed in the U.S.A. Designed by Bookrest. First edition.

Library of Congress Cataloging-in-Publication Data

Wade, Sidney.
Stroke : poems / Sidney Wade.
     p. cm.
"A Karen & Michael Braziller Book."
ISBN 978-0-89255-337-2 (pbk. : alk. paper)
I. Title.

PS3573.A337S77 2008
   811'.54--dc22
2007038375

Contents

No Comfort to Be Had   3

*

Tortoise   7

Snake   8

Poetry and Pleasure   9

Deep Gossip   10

Insurance   11

An Organized Crime-Spree of the Highest Order   13

The Visionary from Apopka   14

An Utterly Gross Thing   16

Metaphysician in the Light   17

Metaphysician in the Dark   18

The Body Politic   19

Time's List of Things to Do   21

Lost Words   22

The Vulgate of Experience   23

*

MONOSONNETS:

Pity the Poor Orange   27

Adam and the Snake Prepare to Recite some Verse   28

After the flood, frogs   29

The Spontaneous Combustion of a Shopkeeper from Alcohol   30

Stroke of Genius   31

*

Siamo a la Frutta   35

Fruit Stand, State Road 301, Waldo, Florida   36

In the Uncertain Light of All We've Seen   37

Ember   38

Leaving Train   39

*

Driving to Assos   43

*

Sexual Blossoms and Their Fierce Addictions   51

Ants and a Little, Vicious Pig   52

Nothing but the Truth   53

Grasping Time by the Collar There's a Point at Which It All Recedes   54

Doomsday Verse   56

Drought   57

Avant-gardening on my weeping knees   58

Q.E.D.   60

No Fact is a Bare Fact   61

Little Pirate Song   62

Six Significant Landscapes and Two Brief Intrigues   63

Long Bright Hall   66

Grand Disastery   68

The Weight of Light   70

*

A Computerized Jet Fountain in the Detroit Metro Airport   73

STROKE

No Comfort to Be Had

After it happened, the blood pressure soared.
Half the body wept, one hand on its brow,
While one of its two legs began to march
To the drum of that which had prevailed.
One half of the brain, bewildered, racked itself
In search of comfort, while the other, firmer
Half scoured the mall for a gown for the ball.

The body, thus arrayed in perfect discord,
One foot crammed in a party shoe, now
Began to stagger around the room, starched
And wilted all at once. One eye, the pale
One, stared at the clock ticking on the shelf
Whose face concealed a belly full of worms.
One hand nailed the mandate to the wall.

November 2004

*

Tortoise

A hollow-eyed head
emerges from this
hard poetic fruit.

The bone mechanic
uproots herself from
an earthen mouth-hole

to graze the thin grass.
Heavy ghost, bland-eyed
child of many wombs,

armored soul, burrowed
darkness visible
and thick, precisely

balances her load
of hungry bone on
four dactylic feet.

Snake

A Rough Green snake daydreams on the bike trail
in the sun, an elegant ribbon of olive light.
We are alone in the world, a solitude of two,
in a formal dimension of our own making, a rite
not of passage but of recognition.
Understood, again, the manumission
Of light to vision. The body translates heat
into form and color—a fine green tale.

Poetry and Pleasure

A vagabond chill
rose up the fire-ramp,
gave me a wink and
a red verb then flew
down the messageway.

Some ravishing words
emerged prettily
from the underwood
and spread themselves on
the black velvet ground.

L'instinct du bonheur
admired their beauty
and was pleasantly
stunned to smell so much
trouble in the air.

Deep Gossip

I

Concerto grosso, blackest heart,
A mystifying natal chart—
All ignite the metaphoric art.

II

A planetful of pure desire
Is all a poet should require
To set the commonplace afire.

III

The heart that hides inside the form
Observes the words that fume and swarm:
No one lives above the storm.

Insurance

for Dorothy Evslin

I'm recklessly flying
my wind-sheared bicycle
no sun-screen no cell phone

I'm loose on the sun-drowned
prairie and chirping *Look
Ma no goddamned helmet*

and Ma at this moment
is standing her fragile-
boned crooked old frame as

straight as she can on the
ledge of her stair-chair and
pushing the button and

rising like a goddess
from the dark undertow
borne upward on a shell

yet bound of course to fall
and it's clear that we need
a policy for when

imagination fails
when an ocean of fact
and white foaming despair

rushes up the hard legs
and submerges the heart
of the headstrong rider

when the tangy salt smell
disaster brings powders
our transported bodies

and threatens our moving
and most always precise
navigations which are

full of prolific doubt
but dazzlingly feathered
and fabulously real

An Organized Crime-Spree of the Highest Order

This just in:
Our apocalyptic nerve gas news analysis team

reports the final dissolution of the Squeamish Party.
The mercantile essence

has reinvigorated the auction-block
and ratcheted up a free-for-all

in our deeply-pocketed hemi-demi-heaven.
Beyond the ever-efflorescent

brass, an occasional lance gleams
in the camps of the foolhardy

who suspect necrosis in the ballot-box
is advanced. Yet the ship of state barges

on, in brilliant rays of tin largesse,
as we mine the metaphysics of the mall.

The Visionary from Apopka

had faith in the largesse of the living
but carried with him
a dozen hand-made urns,
just in case.

He had been born
in a church bathroom
and therefore had a practical habit of mind.
He often organized madrigals at sunset.

I'd had a scuffle with a woman
who had monkey written all over her
and I needed some compound word-matter
to settle my nerves.

How do hew do? I inquired
and he forgave me and gave me his shoes.
You're just in time for the squirm-fest, friend,
he said. *You may also wash your feet.*

I didn't have a forever grant,
but we dealt with that as masterful adults.
We approached the ultimate adding machine
and grabbed us a statue bereft of sin

and some mausoleum gear.
There's not enough shriek and swagger
in our utterly transgressive faith, he confessed,
but he looked down on the others

in their cold, crawling context.
Those people are injured by the time of day,
he sniffed. As we entered a carnelian cloud,
I suggested we leave early and often.

All's well that ends in the dirt, he said.

An Utterly Gross Thing

As principal conjurer of false relief
he traffics in bluff and swagger

and sheds on occasion a single brass tear
The measure of larceny here

is breath-takingly grand
built on blather beyond belief

Our body politic is out of joint
but Dr. K-Mart will see us now and

once we've reached the federally designated turning point
we'll celebrate in gildered streets and golden groves

with the election in the proverbial bag
and random darkness fuming on the stove

Metaphysician in the Light

In the country where she lives,
fat with love and good fortune,
the news arrives every morning
on pure white pages.
She knows the floor of the news factory
is strewn with severed fingers,
rags, and broken teeth.
But here
the sun shines almost every day,
and when it doesn't,
she watches with mild interest
as the foreign torments of rain
surge down the slow-flowing glass
of her spotless windows.

Metaphysician in the Dark

His ancient forehead hung with brittle hair,
he shuffles, bent-kneed, toward the shore.
His eyes shift left to right, wary, bird-like,
as if the flight of vision left him stranded,
silhouetted and exposed on the white
and shifting cataleptic snows of age.
Who let him wander through this place alone?
He's fading in the thinning winter light
and strains to hear, through closed and heavy doors
to inner rooms, inner voices all alike
adrift at sea. They sing their hard and candid
songs of shipwreck and of ice as he stares
across the river, held gently in his cage
of feathered breath, of ever lighter bone.

The Body Politic

Are We in a Slump? We Are . . .

Evil thrives in a variety of plumages—
in protruberant behavior, in brief deceits.

We wander its corridors on the cusp of business,
a mighty fabric over the eyes,

our private darknesses illumined by paraffinalia
and its non-combustible flame,

while the lesser profondeurs blandish and surl
in a controlled burn. It's all map and no shingle.

It's wickedness on fire with bodily intent.
Grotesqueries with a huge probability of failure.

An adroit robbing style with a beau regard.
Rotundity and crenellation.

So their trembling emissary is in a royal jam,
says *get out the way and lissen—*

an apparition at the gate will very soon cast a glance
over your sodden company.

Under that cool cloud over there is a fuming trope,
but it's for the brethren only. And the deputy steppers.

What we are left with is the quantity racket,
muffled illusions, and a very great sadness.

We are dazed and in the open,
on our way to the foreghastly conclusion.

Time's List of Things to Do

Time wants to write a poem
about the metaphorical mind
but first has to fiddle in its pocket
for a pencil.
Outside the window
trees are inching upward
in graceful green increments.
Time is seized by a sense of duty
and writes, instead:

    soup

    sigma

    soap froth

    delta

    volcano

    error

    tau

    then

    smiles

    and

    gently

    wears

    the

    pencil

    down.

Lost Words

The first was *Fair* in all her facets—lovely, pale, and just—a rope of rubies around her doomed and beautiful neck. It was very sad. Next to go was the sturdy and quarrelsome *Equality*, which was a surprise, as we'd known him all these years to be a scrapper. Very soon after that *Truth* and *Charity* suicided themselves off a nearby cliff in despair, or, possibly, in sympathy with the others. These losses have been followed now by those of *Freedom* and *Liberation*, noble and leathery old soldiers, who, in immaculate military dress, faced each other squarely and blew each others' brains out. They left a note, jointly composed and signed, saying they felt duty-bound to remove themselves from further abuse by the authorities. It appears, however, as though a couple of impostors stepped in immediately to take their places and have been circulating glibly ever since.

The Vulgate of Experience

In this tatterdemalion sandwich of Life,
it pays to pay attention to the light,

not to the oligarchic spread of heavy principles,
or to four-week traditions.

There are multitudes caught in the glare
and just as many stuck in a radiant head-book.

The book says even though we might reflect
the bruised glory of all the suns

that ever shone down on the earth,
mostly everyone's dreaming in a savage room

or searching for the beloved in the desert.
I admit I, for one, am clouded by experience,

though I'm feeling my way into a weird pre-waking
from the old parabola of darkness.

Some nights I sleep in wild weather
where the names of God change furiously.

Sometimes I wander in the available light.
The wind is always a perilous distraction.

On rare, sweet days I hear a brown, nut-like sound.
Inside this sound you can hear the imagination fluttering.

Here joy whiskers through the main arteries.
Here is where, if you hold out your hands, they will be filled.

Monosonnets

PITY THE POOR ORANGE

bald
white
orb

on
the
table
rests

its
veined
membrane
exposed

flayed
for
zest

Adam and the Snake Prepare to Recite some Verse

Snake
says

let's
go
mezmerize
some
pomes

Adam
says

I
prefer
to
mammarize
them

AFTER THE FLOOD, FROGS

assemble,
whirp
and
fart,
dissemble,
delve
and
throng,
prolonging
the
agglutinant
song
of
themselves

The Spontaneous Combustion of a Shopkeeper from Alcohol

He
must
have
ignited
red
and
fast

the
crusty
knave
light
spirited
at
last

STROKE OF GENIUS

windfall
display
of
art

playing
a
signal
part

flaying
the
heart

of
indignant
enigma

*

Siamo a la Frutta

It's hot in this red room,
inside the beating heart of the ritual, explosive

now with duress, bleeding its stress
onto the oriental carpet. The salt, little corrosive

grains of light, works its way into the meat.
We talk. We watch. We eat,

our two miracles ingesting the atmosphere between us.
On the table, on a golden plate, the apples bloom.

Fruit Stand, State Road 301, Waldo, Florida

I'm Tard says the sign *No Bidness* is what it means
and we keep driving north through these failing crops

on the untranquil shelf of our personal continent
and the dust lies happy and thick on the dashboard

as thick as under the bed as thick as dirt
when the moral from another poem peeks in

to catch its little breath and gaze with pleasure
on this *tableau vivant* before its tired eyes:

our golden daughter beaming among the motes
and whispering *Hand me that fly swopper got to swop some flies*

In the Uncertain Light of All We've Seen

An abstract notion neared
as I was drawing again your features—

the swollen bell, the verbal annihilations,
the golden socks. It was a creature

of bodily vapors with a dozen interiors,
furnished with ancient chairs,

each one wearier than the next. Lovely and broken.
I saw it till I wrote it and it disappeared.

Ember

what form is this?
this is my hardsong:

fire calls to fire
death to death

and what, then, is left?
ashes and children

an old body unsettling
a new one in the dark

how does it weather?
in brilliant grays

and the medium?
distemper on burnt paper

and how does it end?
in hard-strung dream

red and reddening

Leaving Train

I'm stepping off the Hallelujah Line.
We've rattled down the concourse trunk and hollered
on the bed but now the ties have followed
that wayward track into an unbenign
new distance. Nostalgia bees are fine
when buzzing round a spray of rhododendrons,
but here they sting and bring to life a somber,
vast and achy past. Let's never mind.

I wish we'd known the great highways of love.
Altissimo in seventh gear. The high,
pure dance of sustenance. Here, though, we seem
to founder in the trackless grass. Above
my head a single star wields its light
like a scimitar. I'm on the road. I steam.

*

Driving to Assos

As the road drops
    down from
        the mountains

west of Balıkesir
    and passes
        through Edremit

it turns floral
    coastal
        delicious

the countryside
    is olive-groved
        and gracious

the roadside
    lavishly dressed
        in sunflower

wild hollyhock
    blue and martial
        thistle in windy

light and everywhere
    the radiant blood
       of poppies

the olive trees
    tended and hacked
       as appears

to be necessary
    crouch venerable
       and gray

in the stony
    old groves
       on the shore

    *

Brown towns
    along the way
       are frilled

in roof-high roses
    and hollyhocks spill
       over sidewalks

and farther on
    a holiday village
        simmers in the heat

under a mantle
    of dust and here
        is Kücükküyü

at the countryside's
    ragged edge
        the hillsides far

more bouldery
    than before
        now the road

climbs the hill
    behind Behramkale
        and reaches

the top and the sky
    opens out
        the earth falls

away beneath
    the feet and
        far below green-eyed

Lesbos lazes
    in the hazy
        shimmer of the sea

    *

High among the ruins
    above the shore
        the air bristles

in the thrill of lemon
    thyme and sage
        I am quite alone

except for a herd
    of belled sheep
        tinking and bonging

over the Roman road
    meandering up
        from the sea

here
　　in the middle way
　　　the sun spills

in great sheets
　　into the agora
　　　a slight rustle

betrays a snake
　　gliding across
　　　the trail

it's mythical
　　and still
　　　this golden

earth-bound spirit
　　observes me
　　　with quiet eyes

then whips
　　away through
　　　the brush

and a moment
 later flows back
  across the sun-stroked path .

a liquid omen
 in which I rinse
  all the force

of my manifold
 desires and
  quite

suddenly
 the texture
  of the instant opens

the frame
 it saturates
  the borders

and the light
 of all that's possible
  burns through

*

Sexual Blossoms and Their Fierce Addictions

Yesterday's tulips in the crystal bowl
have begun to open and already they've
partially exposed their pistils and stamens.
In the coming days
these petals will open in a brazen
yawn, their private parts thrust
into the shocked and fascinated
room. Very soon the whole
apartment will start to misbehave—
the fainting couch and ottoman will shed their raiment,
weirdness will graze the ceiling and raise
eyebrows in the carpet lice. With sex emblazoned
on the air, the afflicted chamber will swell with lust.
An hystericalectomy is clearly indicated.

Ants and a Little, Vicious Pig

In a paradigmatic shift in the history
of bloodshed, sacking and carnage,

they liberate the poor from the ferociously horned toad,
then nudge them through harm's gate

and call it a blessing. This immaculate perception
issues from the palaver caravan of a foster human

and follows a great bloating of the vital tongue.
Fat hands are thrust deep into pockets of resistance,

where the vulnerable fling stones,
helpless at the edge of billowing death.

Privilege's minions will keep it swelling,
that rushing and lucrative sorrow river.

Nothing but the Truth

In this ruined word-city, the party is leaking.
The imperatives of the dominant glib prevail

and there's no hope for the culture.
It's monopoloid and tick-rich,

filled with words that will kill you.
I'm burning with passionate shame

for its rear-guard history
and feel all I can do now

is dream by day, drive by night.
But I've got a word-strung gun here,

and it's double-barrelled,
so at least I'm technically focussed. Soon

we will converge on the horrors
with our blind zen-white eyes.

Grasping Time by the Collar
There's a Point at Which It All Recedes

it's time to get it right

get what right?

il mio amore amaro

oh you mean your crippled animal pride

yes the seamless variety that spreads like red mist

ah those ancient transmissions off your body waves

yes it's time to plumb the old passageways and pin it down

ok does it start like this *c'era una volta* . . .

no I don't dwell on the past

ok then *the holy martyrs to the golden flame*

no I think I need to drag the light out from the center
to illuminate those very slender vapors

the red ones with the heavy bones

yes *furioso* and the whole profound illusion

    wild lights! wild lights!

ok but throw me a bone right now I'm a little memory-shy
    and the emerging form is still veiled in brown water

    sigh

Doomsday Verse

In the dying order, they go first,
the little ones. The war heads
have decreed it. They are to be married
to the machinery of death and shepherded
by blank-eyed marshals to the altar.
The power of the powerful will not falter.
Democracy and freedom, etc. etc. etc.
Our vehicles possess a raging thirst.

Drought

In the dessicated lies the windy ones thunder,
in the heat of each day more concentrated in dismay

than the last, while fanatics fan the daily burn
and the social contract withers in disarray,

the dog days dog and the hollow nights fall.
I am helpless to stop them. Instead I sprawl

in this pool of glossy words. They are all I have
to irrigate the old and green and fluent mundo.

Avant-gardening on my weeping knees

tending to the green
immargination of the plot

I tidy up the loose ends of my lines
while all about me twine

the scrollwork and fretwork
of intelligent and perverse design

wing-stroke and piston-stroke
play heartburn music

on the underside of sense
while I pursue

the noble and miserable hounds
of vernacular economics

turning over spadefuls of apparent earth
my fat and vocable wealth

the soil here is the soul
of intelligence

a miracle of steadfastness
in the windy mess

that splatters the whole as I range widely
and with complicated passion

in the dirty possibilities
of the fascinated ground

Q.E.D.

We are serious in the same way,
my catalytic converter and I.
We've flushed my long-term emptiness
down the demi-john and now we mystify
observers with our wild molecular exchange.
Our transported atoms actually rearrange
the nature of heat and light.
Quod Erat Demonstrandum. What more can I say?

No Fact is a Bare Fact

Most are dressed in thermal layers
and some are blessed with Turkish socks.

Take this rib-cage fire—it's gussied up
in ancient finery, an orthodox

fever of the first degree. It's something
stirred up in the body that goes jumping

out into the naked world. Fully clothed.
For your eyes only, *mon* terminal *cher*.

Little Pirate Song

We feeled icky. Words
abuzzed in the sticky air.

The blue profondeur reeled and was rolly.
To a man, we resolved to the stalwart flair,

but instead, we fell toothless.
Toothless and ruthless.

Out on the mezzo-poop deck we admired them sail:
magnificent frigate birds.

Six Significant Landscapes and Two Brief Intrigues

We're jogging down the autumnal foot-path
in a weird little tuning mood.
All the others have vanished
deep into the balsamic woods.

*

See that modern mountain in the distance?
Plow it out of your mind
because the next big thing is out on the plain,
knee-deep in land-funk.

*

There's a clearing in this field
raked by gypsies
who bolted out of the light,
once upon a time.
Blue rain there falls
on the fever-birds.

*

A large red ant
ambles into the woods.
It feels the jagged landscape turning.

*

What we have here
is a foamy pier.
Don't say a word,
or you'll mar the 200-acre glimmer.
Paradise is liquid, you understand.

*

A series of bright animals
verges on the verdant
in overgrown shadow.
They feel in their femurs
an earth-bound tremor.

*

The beauty of the caw
and the stroke of the hammer.
The southern coast
of the southern mystery.
Here in this bondage I thrust out my little eyes.

*

There is no happiness in nature.
Only periphery mayhem.
Then the light seeps in and sweeps things away.

Long Bright Hall

in memory of Karen Klenberg

we're in the hospital now and
Karen is hooked up to the machines
we go in and hold her hand and
say things like *Karen don't die*
Karen your daughters need you
Karen your hair looks great
and our words wash over her
great bloated white body like
water and then evaporate
and then she dies

we're a crowd in this hall heavy
and helpless as a beached whale
we're stunned we start to cry
and a woman who's been waiting
in the same hall for days and praying
for her own daughter in a coma
bows her head and closes her eyes
Jesus hold her hand Jesus help them
in their grief Jesus Lord have mercy on her soul
she was fine one slender
week ago and now she's done

and now the family dazes out the door
of the death room in a hard tight knot
and we clench even harder

our faces bald and wet with grief
for them and for our Karen gone
all numb in the humming florescent lights
stalled and empty in this harshly
illuminated hall this artery
whose bright currents feed that great
dark body made of earth and shadow

Grand Disastery

moored by fine
tethers to certain death

a hornet fizzes
on the windowsill

a spider flies
to its side

to securely bind
this abundant harvest

the hornet in shrill
thrall to agony drills

a hole in God's
provident breast

pocket
in the sublime

cold light
of this tiny

constellation
the bald pulp

of the hornet's diminishing
hum feeds growing eyes

and hungry sockets
the figure is clean

a small
black aster

hung among
the stars

The Weight of Light

We sit on a bench in the park,
you and I and the sliver
of distance we carry between us,
and your eyes fill with the weight
of the perfect light we've been given to bear.
The sun shines inside each leaf of every tree
and on their trunks and through each blade of autumn grass.

The world outside this illumined order is dark,
as it always is, which makes our portion even lovelier.
In this moment, sowing its great and murderous
swindle overseas, the state
efficiently removes the available light from the air
of thousands of darkened rooms. The economy
requires it. We hold each other fast.

*

A Computerized Jet Fountain in the Detroit Metro Airport

to Richard Wilbur

Perfect tubes of water,
shot from hidden modern grottoes, their flat
cylinder heads drily intact,
leap and curve, swift and sleek as otters

and equally alive,
as if they sported minds of their own and knew
exactly where they had to get to
and when. Their muscularly perfect dive

into the flat, shining
mirror of the surface that receives them
is a miracle of theorem,
mathematical and clean, at once defining

joy and pure control.
The parabolic arches made of time
and pressure express the delicious rhyme
of flight and landing, melting in the bowl

of sure return, the end
its own beginning. The fullness of desire
frolics here in fluid attire
and recognizes, even as it bends

in play, the underside
of bliss, in polished granite, adamant and black.
We travellers will end up back
where we began, and may our gods provide

us all with equal grace
and fluent spirit on our way, even
if our paths won't chart the heaven
towards which all hungers leap, all pleasures race.